I0457458

Thank You Jesus

For Life Beyond This Life

written & illustrated by Darcy Jackson

Thank You Jesus For Life Beyond This Life
Copyright © 2023 Darcy Jackson
All rights reserved.
ISBN: 978-1-990871-078 (paperback)
        978-1-990871-085 (epub)

Published by Fictitious Ink Publishing, Tumbler Ridge,
BC, Canada, V0C 2W0

No part of this book may be reproduced in any form or
by any electronic or mechanical means, including
information storage and retrieval systems, without
written permission from the author, except for the use of
brief quotations in a book review.

Scripture quotations are taken from the Holy Bible, New
International Version®, NIV®. Copyright © 1973, 1978,
1984, 2011 by Biblica, Inc.™ Used by permission of
Zondervan. All rights reserved worldwide. www.zonder-
van.com The "NIV" and "New International Version" are
trademarks registered in the United States Patent and
Trademark Office by Biblica, Inc.™

This booklet is
devoted to Lord Jesus
and dedicated to my friend and sister
Shauna.
You are an overcomer!
I ❤️ you,
DarcyL

Philippians 2 : 13

"...for it is God
who works in you
to will and to act
according to
His good purpose."

The book of Philippians:
St. Paul's later letter from prison.
A message of potential 'goodbye' and
Hope for a glorious Life beyond this
earthly existence of pain and suffering.
Grace and Peace
to all who are longing for a
Better Day!
With love in Christ,
DarcyL

Philippians 1 : 2
Grace and Peace to you
from God our Father
and the Lord Jesus Christ.

5

Philippians 1 : 6
I am confident of this;
that He who began a good work in you
will carry it on to completion
until the Day of
Christ Jesus.

Thank You Jesus
that you are still working
in me

Philippians 1 : 9, 10, 11
This is my prayer:
that your love may abound
more and more in
knowledge and depth of insight,
so that you may be able to discern
what is best and may be pure and
blameless until the Day of Christ,
filled with the fruit of
righteousness that comes through
Jesus Christ -
to the glory and praise of God.

*Thank You Jesus
that Your love abounds in me*

Philippians 1 : 20, 21
I eagerly expect and hope that
I will in no way be ashamed, but
will have sufficient courage so that
now as always, Christ will be
exalted in my body,
whether by life or by death.
For to me, to live is Christ
and to die is gain!

To live is Christ and to die is gain!

11

Philippians 2 : 1, 2
If you have any encouragement from
being united with Christ,
if any comfort from His Love,
if any fellowship with the Spirit,
if any tenderness and compassion,
then make my joy complete by
being like-minded,
having the same love,
being one in Spirit and purpose.

13

Philippians 2 : 5 - 8
Your attitude should be the same
as that of Christ Jesus:
Who, being in very nature God,
did not consider equality with God
something to be grasped, but
made Himself nothing, taking the very
nature of a servant,
being made in human likeness.
And being found in appearance as a man,
He humbled Himself and became
obedient to death -
even death on a cross!

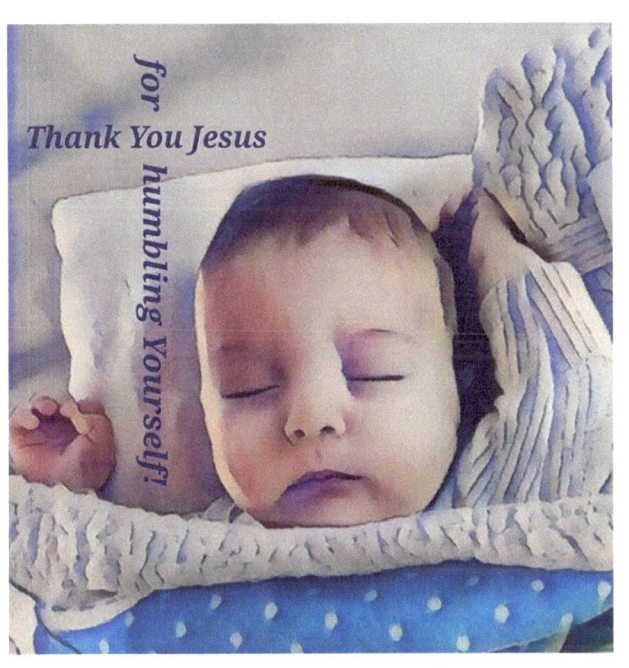

15

Philippians 2 : 9 - 11
Therefore, God exalted Him to the
highest place and gave Him the Name
that is above every name;
that at the Name of Jesus
every knee should bow
in heaven and on earth
and under the earth,
and every tongue confess that
Jesus Christ is Lord,
to the glory of God the Father!

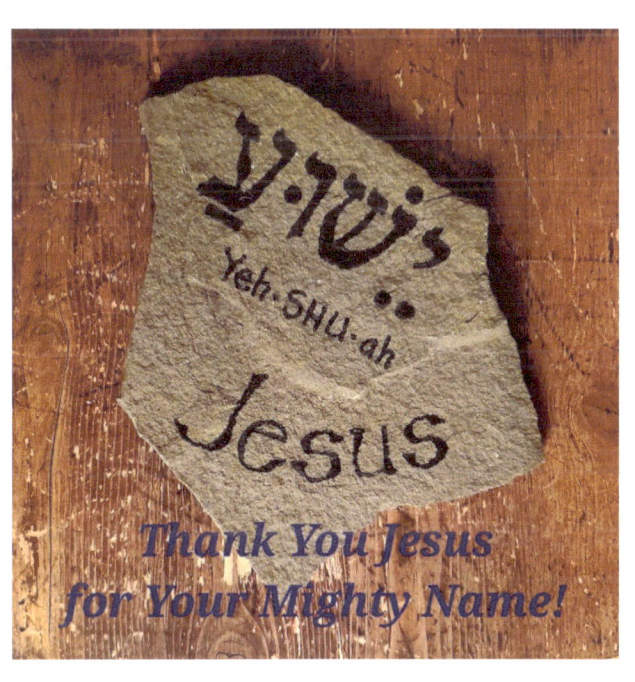

יֵשׁוּעַ

Yeh·SHU·ah

Jesus

**Thank You Jesus
for Your Mighty Name!**

Philippians 2 : 14 - 16
Do everything without complaining
or arguing, so that you may
become blameless and pure
children of God, without fault in a
crooked and depraved generation,
in which you shine like stars
in the universe
as you hold out the
Word of Life!

Philippians 3 : 7, 8, 9
Whatever was to my profit, I now
consider loss for the sake of Christ.
What is more, I consider everything a
loss compared to the surpassing greatness
of knowing Christ Jesus my Lord, for
Whose sake I have lost all things.
I consider them rubbish, that I may
gain Christ and be found in Him;
not having a righteousness of my own
that comes from the law, but that which is
through faith in Christ - the righteousness
that comes from God and is by faith.

Thank You Jesus

for Your surpassing greatness. All else is rubbish in comparison.

Philippians 3 : 10, 11
I want to know Christ and the
power of His Resurrection
and the fellowship of sharing in
His sufferings, becoming like Him
in His death, and so, somehow,
to attain to the resurrection
from the dead.

Thank You Jesus for *Your Resurrection Power*

Philippians 3 : 12, 13, 14
Not that I have already obtained all this,
or have already been made perfect,
but I press on to take hold of that
for which Christ Jesus took hold of me.
I do not consider myself yet
to have taken hold of it.
But one thing I do;
forgetting what is behind, and
straining toward what is ahead,
I press on toward the goal to win the prize
for which God has called me
heavenward in Christ Jesus!

Thank You Jesus for my heavenly goal

Philippians 3 : 20, 21
Our citizenship is in heaven, and
we eagerly await a Savior from there,
the Lord Jesus Christ,
who, by the power that enables Him
to bring everything under His control,
will transform our lowly bodies
so that they will be like
His glorious body!

Philippians 4 : 4, 5
Rejoice in the Lord always!
I will say it again: Rejoice!
Let your gentleness
be evident to all.
The Lord is near.

Thank You Jesus
for times of rejoicing

Philippians 4 : 6, 7
Do not be anxious about anything,
but in everything,
by prayer and petition, with thanksgiving,
present your requests to God.
And the peace of God,
which transcends all understanding,
will guard your hearts
and your minds
in Christ Jesus.

Thank You Jesus
for Your Peace

31

Philippians 4 : 8, 9
Whatever is true, whatever is noble,
whatever is right, whatever is pure,
whatever is lovely, whatever is admirable,
if anything is excellent
or praiseworthy -
think about such things.
Whatever you have learned or
received or heard from me,
or seen in me -
put it into practice.
And the God of peace will be with you.

Philippians 4 : 12, 13
I know what it is to be in need, and
I know what it is to have plenty.
I have learned the secret of being content
in any and every situation,
whether well fed or hungry,
whether living in plenty or in want.
I can do all things
through Him who gives me strength.

Thank You Jesus

for feeding my soul

Philippians 4 : 19, 20
My God will meet all your needs
according to His glorious riches
in Christ Jesus.
To our God and Father
be glory for ever and ever.
Amen.

Philippians 4 : 23
The grace of the Lord Jesus Christ
be with your spirit.
Amen.

I am a child of God
I AM
saved by grace
redeemed by Jesus
loved & forgiven

39

40

Father in Heaven,
Thank You that You love me so much!
Lord Jesus Christ,
Thank You that You died for me
so I could be forgiven and set free.
I receive Your forgiveness
And I say "Yes!" to Your invitation
to have a relationship with You.
I turn away from my bad choices and
I put my faith and hope in You.
Holy Spirit,
I ask You to fill my heart with
Your Presence.
Thank You in the Name of Jesus,
Amen.

More in the series!

We hope you found this inspirational
pocketbook uplifting. The simple
affirmative statements, illustrations,
and scriptures were prayerfully compiled
by the author to bring you
strength and peace.

Plus, there are more books in the series!
They'd make a beautiful gift for someone
you love. Available at select bookstores
and online. God bless!

*If you enjoyed this book, please consider
leaving a positive rating or review.*

www.ingramcontent.com/pod-product-compliance
Lightning Source LLC
Chambersburg PA
CBHW040905120626
46551CB00006B/658

* 9 7 8 1 9 9 0 8 7 1 0 7 8 *